# LOVE and DREAM

## Japanese Art Calligraphy

BY

# Koshu

　この世に命をもらった瞬間から、人生の物語の小節ごとに必要な大切な出逢いを与えてもらえてきた。幸福を共鳴し合う出逢い、成長するのに大切な学びとしての出逢い、困難を乗り越えるのに勇気や支えとなる出逢い、次に進む道への導きへの出逢い…。『我逢人』人生はまさに出逢いだと思う。

　八歳で書の筆に出逢い、歩み始めた道。数々の大切な出逢いのお陰で人生が深まり、心の奥で感じたままを、手に取った筆が舞うように表現できる私になれた。それは『心が満たされる喜び』を体感できる瞬間であり、私の人生において特別な贈り物だと感じている。

　この紅秋作品集は、受けた愛に感謝し、注ぐ愛に喜びを感じ、夢を追い輝く心を持つ事で、次の大切な出逢いを導いていく：『愛と夢』と言うメッセージをタイトルに、私の人生の過去、現在、そして未来の出逢いに感謝の気持ちを込めて表現した数々の作品を集め制作された。

　今この瞬間が書道家『紅秋』としての新たなスタート。 更に出逢い豊かな大空に羽ばたけるように夢を見続け、舞い続け、表現し続けたいと思う。

　紅秋作品集『愛と夢』を手に取り見て下さる方々と、作品を通して何か共感できるものがあれば大変嬉しく思います。ありがとうございます。

平成二十五年十一月

紅秋：ルーカス明美

I have been given so many precious opportunities to meet those who are so dear to me since I was gifted with my life in this world; meeting someone to share my joy, meeting someone to learn from, meeting someone who can mutually give me courage or support, and meeting someone who could lead me to the next step in this journey of life... I believe in the saying "Gahojin" (see page 24): The most important thing in your life is whom you meet.

Since I encountered the world of calligraphy, and since I started to hold a brush, I have learnt so much. I have learnt from all those people I have met. They have deepened my life and provided it with significance, leading to what I have achieved now: being able to express my heart through my brush, as it dances on the paper. This gift, being able to experience this special moment, is so fulfilling and blissful for me.

This book of my art expresses the gratitude I feel to all those I have met in the past, present, and those who I am going to meet in the future. The title "Love and Dream" has a significant message, and all my artwork evolves around this theme; the title has connotations to appreciating the love you are given, to feel joy to give your love, and having a dream which will make you shine and attract those around you, leading you to meet another precious person in your life.

This moment is my next stage as a calligrapher, Koshu. I would love to carry on dreaming, carry on making my brush dance, and to continue my journey to where I am destined to be; expressing myself to each and every one I meet on my journey, hoping to shine in their lives.

Thank you so much for looking at this book. I hope that my message and feelings can be shared to you through my artwork.

Koshu : Akemi Lucas
November 2013

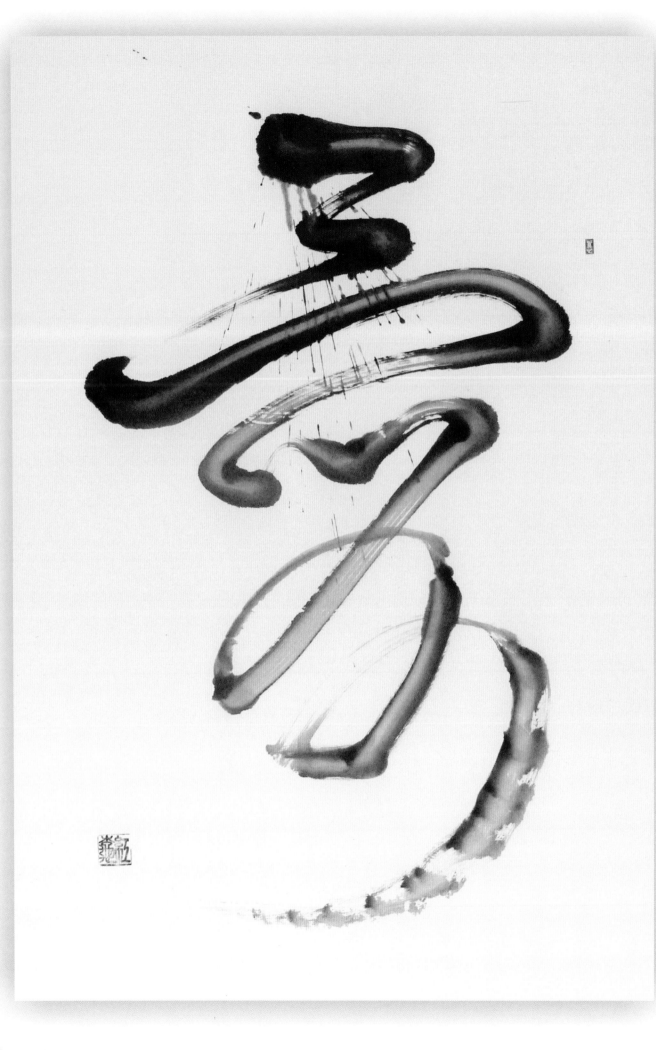

(to the left)

## 『愛』 "LOVE"

宇宙のどこからとも無く届く果てしない愛、過去から未来から時を越え届く人々からの愛、ぎゅっと抱きしめて触れて感じる愛…。
受けた愛に感謝し、注ぐ愛に喜びを感じることで、人と人を繋ぎ調和を生み出すことができる。

Eternal love encloses us from everywhere. From the inner core of the Universe to the outer layer of the Universe. From the past, and from the future. The love we endure now is the love we feel now. The love I felt then has been expressed through this piece. Appreciating the love you were given, feeling joy to give your love.
This is that will connect every other and bring harmony and peace.

190 x 110 cm

## 『夢』 "DREAM"

目覚めたら儚く消える夢、だから後悔無く生き抜いていく。
未来に向かって希望を持ち、夢を見ることで、魅力的に輝く心が次への大切な出逢いを導いていく。

There are some dreams you see at night, and some that you hope for, for the future. Despite some disappear as you awake, other dreams are there for you to chase. These dreams will make you shine, attracting all those around you; this is what will lead you to the one for your next step in your journey.

131 x 57.5 cm

『龍飛鳳舞』 ”Dragon”

龍も鳳凰も想像上の動物で、龍は力強く高く飛ぶ男性
の、鳳凰は 優雅に舞う女性の姿を象徴し、不可能だと思
える事柄を可能にしていく運気を転換し大望を成就す
る。

**Dragon flies, Phoenix dances**

The magnificent creatures, the dragon and the phoenix are
myths.  Yet they cam make the impossible happen.  If the
dragon symbolized man, flying powerfully, the phoenix will
symbolize woman, gracefully dancing; and together they
will form peace and bring good fortune.

Scroll 280 x 71 cm

『鸞翔鳳集』 ”Ran Bird: Fabulous Mythical Bird”

優れた才能を持った人が集まり来るという意味。
鸞は神鳥、神 霊の精が鳥と化したといわれる。鸞や鳳凰
が飛ぶときにはその徳によって嵐も雷も起こらず、河川
も漏れず草木も揺れず、他の鳥もその後をついて飛び、
死ねば多くの鳥が嘆き悲しんだという。
聖天使の治める平和な世のみ姿を現す特別な鳥。

**It is time for the Gifted people to fly and get together.**

As the Ran flies, so does the Phoenix. As the Phoenix flies,
so does every other bird. They bring peace to all creatures
and nature will withdraw to its power. They will also cause
storms to cease and pause nature's movement. The power
of the Ran could be seen as holy and as the spirit of God,
symbolically representing how those gifted, will come
together and bring worldly peace.

Scroll 280 x 71 cm

天地玄黃　宇宙洪荒　日月盈昃　辰宿列張　寒來暑往　秋收冬藏　閏餘成歲　律呂調陽　雲騰致雨　露結為霜　金生麗水　玉出崑岡　劍號巨闕　珠稱夜光　果珍李柰　菜重芥薑　海鹹河淡　鱗潛羽翔　龍師火帝　鳥官人皇　始制文字　乃服衣裳　推位讓國　有虞陶唐　弔民伐罪　周發殷湯　坐朝問道　垂拱平章　愛育黎首　臣伏戎羌　遐邇壹體　率賓歸王　鳴鳳在樹　白駒食場　化被草木　賴及萬方　蓋此身髮　四大五常　恭惟鞠養　豈敢毀傷　女慕貞絜　男效才良　知過必改　得能莫忘　罔談彼短　靡恃己長　信使可覆　器欲難量　墨悲絲染　詩讚羔羊　景行維賢　克念作聖　德建名立　形端表正　空谷傳聲　虛堂習聽　禍因惡積　福緣善慶　尺璧非寶　寸陰是競　資父事君　曰嚴與敬　孝當竭力　忠則盡命　臨深履薄　夙興溫凊　似蘭斯馨　如松之盛　川流不息　淵澄取映　容止若思　言辭安定　篤初誠美　慎終宜令　榮業所基　籍甚無竟　學優登仕　攝職從政　存以甘棠　去而益詠　樂殊貴賤　禮別尊卑　上和下睦　夫唱婦隨　外受傅訓　入奉母儀　諸姑伯叔　猶子比兒　孔懷兄弟　同氣連枝　交友投分　切磨箴規　仁慈隱惻　造次弗離　節義廉退　顛沛匪虧　性靜情逸　心動神疲　守真志滿　逐物意移　堅持雅操　好爵自縻　都邑華夏　東西二京　背邙面洛　浮渭據涇　宮殿盤鬱　樓觀飛驚　圖寫禽獸　畫綵仙靈　丙舍傍啟　甲帳對楹　肆筵設席　鼓瑟吹笙　升階納陛　弁轉疑星　右通廣內　左達承明　既集墳典　亦聚群英　杜稿鍾隸　漆書壁經　府羅將相　路俠槐卿　戶封八縣　家給千兵　高冠陪輦　驅轂振纓　世祿侈富　車駕肥輕　策功茂實　勒碑刻銘　磻溪伊尹　佐時阿衡　奄宅曲阜　微旦孰營　桓公匡合　濟弱扶傾　綺回漢惠　說感武丁　俊乂密勿　多士寔寧　晉楚更霸　趙魏困橫　假途滅虢　踐土會盟　何遵約法　韓弊煩刑　起翦頗牧　用軍最精　宣威沙漠　馳譽丹青　九州禹跡　百郡秦并　嶽宗恆岱　禪主云亭　雁門紫塞　雞田赤城　昆池碣石　鉅野洞庭　曠遠綿邈　巖岫杳冥　治本於農　務茲稼穡　俶載南畝　我藝黍稷　稅熟貢新　勸賞黜陟　孟軻敦素　史魚秉直　庶幾中庸　勞謙謹敕　聆音察理　鑑貌辨色　貽厥嘉猷　勉其祗植　省躬譏誡　寵增抗極　殆辱近恥　林皋幸即　兩疏見機　解組誰逼　索居閒處　沈默寂寥　求古尋論　散慮逍遙　欣奏累遣　慼謝歡招　渠荷的歷　園莽抽條　枇杷晚翠　梧桐早凋　陳根委翳　落葉飄颻　遊鯤獨運　凌摩絳霄　耽讀玩市　寓目囊箱　易輶攸畏　屬耳垣牆　具膳餐飯　適口充腸　飽飫烹宰　飢厭糟糠　親戚故舊　老少異糧　妾御績紡　侍巾帷房　紈扇圓潔　銀燭煒煌　晝眠夕寐　藍筍象床　弦歌酒讌　接杯舉觴　矯手頓足　悅豫且康　嫡後嗣續　祭祀蒸嘗　稽顙再拜　悚懼恐惶　箋牒簡要　顧答審詳　骸垢想浴　執熱願涼　驢騾犢特　駭躍超驤　誅斬賊盜　捕獲叛亡　布射僚丸　嵇琴阮嘯　恬筆倫紙　鈞巧任釣　釋紛利俗　並皆佳妙　毛施淑姿　工顰妍笑　年矢每催　曦暉朗曜　璇璣懸斡　晦魄環照　指薪修祜　永綏吉劭　矩步引領　俯仰廊廟　束帶矜莊　徘徊瞻眺　孤陋寡聞　愚蒙等誚　謂語助者　焉哉乎也

行書千字文

平成六年甲戌之夏　紅秋書

## 『千字文』
### "A Thousand Chinese Characters"

楷書（左）Regular style (left)
行書（中央）Semi-running style (middle)
草書（右）Running style (right)

千字文は重複しない一千字の漢字。
天理、地理、政治、経済、社会、歴史、倫理などの森羅
万象について述べた四字一句、二百五十個の短句からな
る韻文書。西暦500年に作られ日本へは聖徳太子の時代
に伝わる。
（臨書作品）

A Poem with a thousand characters made in China in 500 AD.
None of the characters are repeated. One phrase contains 4 characters each and makes 250 phrases, describing the whole creation of the Universe.
It arrived in Japan in around 600 AD.

Scroll 196 x 73 cm

『福寿』
**"Good fortune & Long life"**

貴方の人生が幸福であり、
長命でありますように。。。

For your life to be fulfilled with
happiness and continue to eternity.

Scroll 138 x 71 cm

**『囲碁将棋道場』**
看板用

**"IGO & SHOGI SCHOOL"**
Sign Board for Japanese Chess (IGO & SHOGI) School

44 x 172 cm

**『鈴泉釜』**
看板用

**"REISEN GAMA"**
Sign Board for Japanese Pottery Studio

60 x 140 cm

10

(to the left)

## 『覚』 "The Sleepers must awaken"

眠っている人たち、今目覚める時が来た。心をとらえていた迷いを捨て、潜んでいた感情、知能、本能全てを認識し、隠された才能を発揮するときが来た。

Come out of your hidden place.
Appear from your discreetness.
Awaken from your sleep.
Awaken your inner sense of self, and your hidden talent.
Awaken your senses and realize your path out of the dark towards the light.
The time has come, for those sleeping gifts, to awaken.

163 x 110 cm

## 『愛結集の時』 "Time for love"

地球の為に、世界の為に、未来の為に、今一人一人の意識を変えて『愛』を向けていく時が来た。
『愛』が結集された瞬間、きっと奇跡が起きると信じて…。

For the earth, For the world, and for the future; the time has come to change each ones mind and to bring love together.
Believe that a miracle will happen when love will come together.

122 x 48 cm

『海闊天空』
"Kaikatutenku"

海や空がきわまりなく広がっているように、
広々として度量が大きく何のわだかまりもない心を持つ人になれるに。
また言葉や発想などにも限りを持つ事無く自由に広げていけるように。

As the ocean has no end, the sky ascends so high.
Open your mind, and don't limit yourself.
Broaden your views and be generous without prejudice.
Finally, let your imagination run free and expand endlessly.

70 x 131 cm

『親心』 "Love from Parents"

『親思う心にまさる親心けふの訪れなんと聞くらん』

子が親を思う気持ち以上に親の子に対する慈愛の気持ちは強く深い。
自分が親になって初めてその気持ちが分かる。

吉田松蔭詩

A child may believe they care for their parents,
yet the power of love a parent can hold for their child has no comparison.
This can only be understood once the child is put in the same position.

Poem by Shoin Yoshida

70 x 136 cm

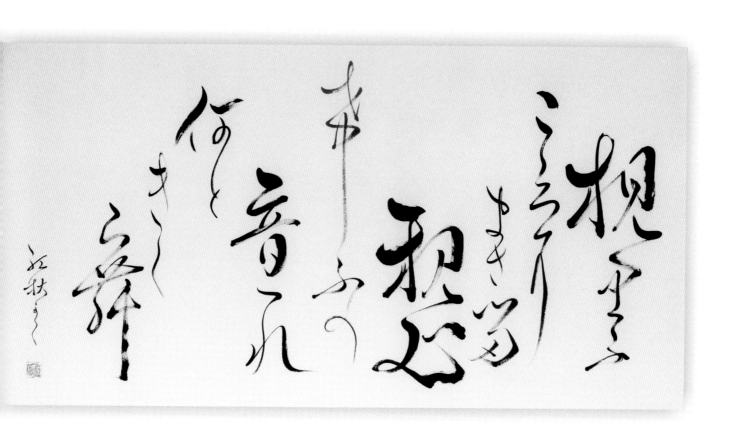

**『愛は命の源』** "Love is the source of life"

愛があるからこそ生きていける。愛には終わりは無く、無限の勇気を与えてくれる。
そして愛は奇跡さえ起こせる力を持っている。

Love is the start of life. It is the necessity for all and is the motivation to live.
Love can forget limits, and give you courage endlessly, so love can cause miracles.

136 x 70 cm

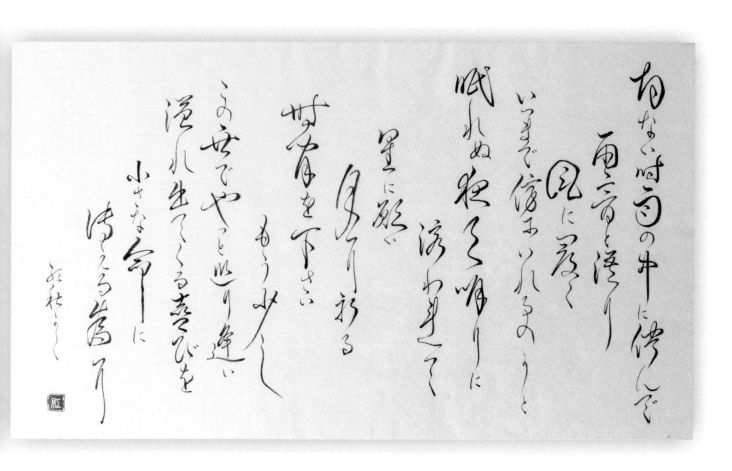

## 『父親になって』
### "Love to my daughter, from a Father's Heart"

切ないとき雨の中に佇んで
雨音と語り
風に尋く
いつまで傍にいれるのかと
眠れる夜月明かりに誘われて
星に願い
月に祈る
時間を下さいもう少し
この世でやっと巡り逢い
溢れ出てくる喜びを
小さな命に伝える為に

紅秋詩

Standing under the crying clouds,
Talking to the rain.
Asking the breeze
"How much longer can I be with her?"
Sleepless nights pass, whilst I'm drawn into to the moonlight.
Wishing to the stars and
Praying to the moon.
"Please gift me with just a little bit more time;
time to express my over flowing emotions.
For I at last met her in this immense world.
I finally became a father for this precious new life.

Poem by Koshu

34 x 59 cm

『阿吽』 "AUN"

相手を馬鹿にしていては生まれない呼吸のように
物事が始まる時から終わるまでの呼吸が簡潔でバランスが完璧。
理屈や説明さえ何もいらないほどの信頼と理解があること。
陰と陽のバランスのように。

The chemistry between him and me is perfect.
We can connect through a silent conversation.
No need for words, no need for reasons, and no need for explanations.
As from the beginning to the end, we understand each other,
we respect each other, and we trust each other, as we are one together,
like the Yin & Yang.

45 x 70 cm

## 『遍界不曽蔵』 "Looking Deeply"

目が曇っていたり、心が閉ざされていると真実が見えなくなる。
見えない物が実は大切。よく見れば真実は見える。
よく見る目を養う事、良く感じる心を養う事が大切。

< 禅の言葉 >

If your hearts door is shut, or if you have closed your eyes,
you have limited the truth.
Yet through the realization, you can open the door or open your eyes to see
and enhance the truth.
It is important for you to have the eyes to see the truth,
and realise your true colours.

< From Zen >

48 x 121 cm

『白いひかり』 "White Light"

何千年もの歴史を経て
光と共に扉が開く
仲間たちとの再会
恐怖からの解放
貴方の勇気と深愛に
世界が喜び深まる絆
ありがとう、愛の音
ありがとう、白い光

2012 年春　紅秋詩

After a thousand years of history,
finally the door opens with the light.
Cross the bridge towards the people you were looking for
Make them free from their fear.
Your courage and deep love will bring
happiness and connections to the world.
Thank you so much, sound of love.
Thank you so much, the white light.

Spring 2012  Poem by Koshu

39 x 66cm

## 『誠実』 ”Sincerity”

私利私欲をまじえず、真心をもって人や物事にたいする心。
誠実な心、誠実な態度、誠実な生き方ができる人で有りたい。

Do not let your ego and greed pervade your actions.  Express your true heart and
your true colours to confront each other and every situation.  Your humble heart,
your humble attitude, and your humble ways to live are what you should express.

68 x 35 cm

## 『輝: 人生まさに出逢、笑顔そして感謝』
### "SHINE : In life, what is important is whom you meet.  Smile and Appreciation"

幸福を共鳴し合う出逢い、成長するのに大切な学びとしての出逢い、困難を乗り越えるのに勇気や支えとなる出逢い、次に進む道への導きへの出逢い。出逢いによって人生は深まり、笑顔と感謝で接していける心を忘れずにいることで『輝き』を持つ人になれる。

Meeting someone to share your joy, meeting someone to learn from, meeting someone who can mutually give you courage or support, and meeting someone who could lead you to the next step in this journey.  In life, what is important is whom you meet, and how you can reflect with them.  Never forget your smile, as that is what creates another smile.  Never forget to appreciate all you have and all you know, as it will be too late once they have disappeared.  If so, you will achieve who you want to be and shine in the life of others.

70 x 46 cm

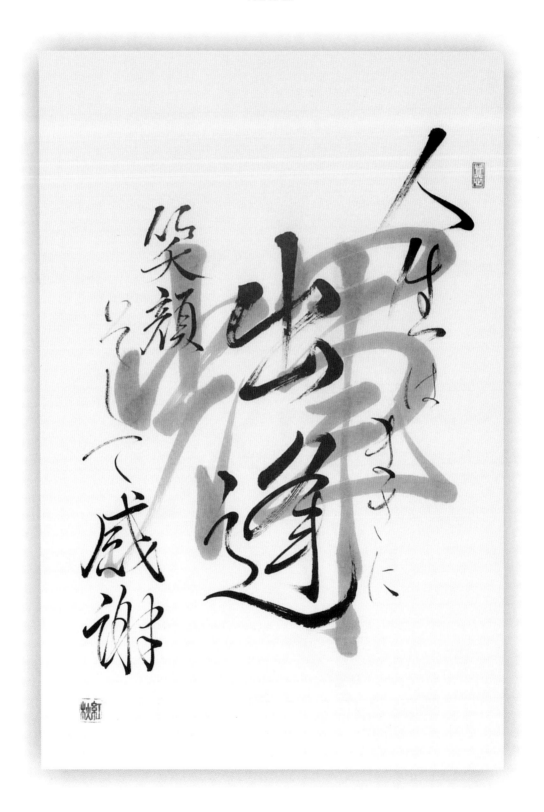

### 『曹源一滴水』 ”One drop of water”

一滴の水が大河となる可能性がある。人間一人一人にはとてつもない可能性がある。
一滴一滴の水を大切に、一人一人の命、可能性を大切に。

< 禅の言葉 >

One drop of water can make a ripple, large enough to create an ocean.
One person can create the ripple, large enough to change the world.

< From Zen >

69 x 68 cm

『奇跡』 ”Miracle”

今が大切な時。今こそ奇跡を呼び起こす時。奇跡がきっと何かを変えてくれる。
一人一人の人生だったり、宇宙全体の流れだったり。

The time has come, the time to make a miracle; A miracle to change the life of man.
A miracle to change the Universe.

70 x 45 cm

## 『鼓動』 "Heart Beat"

生きてる『鼓動』命のサウンドがビートしてる。
耳を澄まして聞いてみて、貴方の心に響きわたり広がる大切な命。

Your heartbeat is the sound of life. Open your ears and listen to the beat as it echoes within you;
for that is the source of what gives us our treasured life.

70 x 45 cm

『鼓動』 "Heart Beat"

**『我逢人』 "GAHOJIN"**

人と人との出逢いの尊さ。心と心の出逢い、物と物との出逢い、人と物との出逢い、出逢いこそ命。
構えた格好でも些細な偶然でも人との出逢いは何かを生み出す。人は自分とは違う領域を持って生きている。
だから出逢いによって広く深く成長させてくれる。人と出逢う事を大切に、人に出逢える場を大切に、人と出逢
う姿を大切に。　　　　　　　　　　　　　　　＜禅の言葉＞

Treasure every person you meet and appreciate all who come into your life. Even if it's coincidental for you to meet, or even if it's arranged for you to meet, treasure it; as they will still bring you something new. They will have different knowledge, different perspectives, and will have experienced different things. Learn from them, and mature into a considerate being, carrying all good aspects of those whom you meet. Treasure who you meet. Treasure where you meet them. And treasure how you meet them.　　<Zen Word>

68 x 35 cm

**『紅の秋 もみじ』** ”Autumn”

恋しく思う、情熱的な日本の秋の紅葉の美しさ

“Red Autumn” symbolic of the passionate beauty with connotations to the diversity of colours in Japanese Autumn.

52 x 36 cm

『意識』 "ISHIKI"

自分自身の心の奥を見つめて感じる。
その奥の意識を曇らせてしまうのか、
それとも晴天の状態にするのかは自分
次第、そこにいつも真実があるはず。

In order to understand yourself, look into
the infinite layers, which create your
sense of self.  Look into your inner heart,
as that is where the truth lies.
Yet it is your choice, whether to decide if
your heart will be cloudy or clear.

68 x 35 cm

## 『幸せの道はここより梅花』
### "Plum Flower"

**The path towards happiness is here,
started just by a Plum Tree.**

梅の花の匂いと美しさが長い冬の終わ
りを告げるように、まるで人生の幸せ
への道へ導いてくれるかのようだ。

歳時記　谷崎吐光詩

After a dark and cold winter, the plum
flower will bring us the fragrance of
Spring, and lead you towards the path of
peace and happiness.

From Saijiki

85 x 35 cm

### 『月のひかりとの共鳴』 ”Moon Light”

月からのひかり (愛、エネルギー) はいつも貴方に注いでいて、
貴方が心の器を広げ、想い (愛) を向けたとき、
月と貴方との愛の共鳴 (受け渡し) ができる。
なにか神秘的な物語が始まるのでは。月にありがとう。

The moonlight showers energy, which always surrounds us.
Yet the energy can only be received once you are in the right state of mind,
and once you have interacted with the moon.
This will become the beginning of your own magical tale.

54 x 113 cm  (to the top)
35 x 68 cm  (to the bottom)

**『信じきる心そこには愛』**
**"Trust; there will be love"**

誰かを心から信じきれる時そこには不安も失う物も無い。
全てを受け入れて委ねられる、
そこには深い愛があるから。

Once you devote your sincere trust, then there will be love.
Trust is a source of love, and love leads to trust.

45 x 70 cm

### 『喜怒哀楽』
#### "Emotions"

辛さや悲しみで心が苦しい時、
感じる心を失いたいと望む。
何も感じない心を持ちたいと望む。
でも心があるから貴方の人生がある。
楽しんで怒って泣いて感動して
きっと生きる喜びを感じていける日がまたやってくる。

When you feel as though your grief is endless and so deep,
you sometimes feel as if you will live the rest of your life
transfixed without emotion or hope.
But gradually, the time will come for this icy grief to melt away
and room will appear for your feelings to plant its seeds again.

35 x 130 cm

『希望』 "Hope"

たとえ果てしない暗闇の中にいようとも希望は常に潜んでいる。
希望の光は腕を広げて暗闇から引き出そうとしてくれて、
必要な場所へ導いてくれる。
希望を持ち、夢を見る心があるから人は輝ける。

Even if you're hidden under infinite layers of darkness,
hope will always exist.
Light of hope will stretch its arm out and pull you out of your darkness,
and lead you to your destined place.

32 x 23 cm

### 『生』 "Meaning of Life"

与えられた尊い命、尊い人生、尊い時間。
誰もがそれぞれ違う人生を与えられ、違う人生を歩む。
どうして？なぜ？って疑問は尽きず、人生の意味を探究し続ける。
与えられた人生を受け入れ、感謝し、一瞬一瞬を大切に後悔無く過ごし、
輝ける人生にしていきたい。

We are all given a precious life, a precious path of life, a precious time for life.
No one has the same life, and on one walks the same path.
Why? How? Metaphysical questions pervade us to search the meaning of life.
Yet all we can do is appreciate, cherish, and accept who we are,
and treasure every moment in life with no regrets.
Make your given life shine.

*46 x 35cm*

## 『尊い命：命の尊さを知ったとき愛する心にこころが届く』
### "Precious Life"

実際に命がどんなに尊い物なのか、
その命との出逢いがどれだけ尊い物なのかに気づいたとき、
自分の奥底にある
『愛する心』に心が届き人生の意味の扉が開く

Once you realise the importance of life,
once you understand how precious this gift is,
this is finally when your heart can realise all the love you have felt.

35 x 85 cm

『愛』"Love" (top) & 『勇敢』"Bravery" (bottom)

人生、何度も勇気が必要な場面に直面する。
勇気を振り絞る瞬間必要なのは愛。
そして勇敢な行為の奥には深い愛が有るからできる。

In life, we often face moments, which force us to be courageous.
To be courageous, we need the motivation by love;
and so your deep love for others can evoke your bravery.

35 x 46cm

**『卒業証書』 Japanese Graduation Certificate**
楷書体の賞状（見本用）

Regular Style Certificate
29 x 41cm

**『祝詞』 Japanese Certificate**
行書体の賞状（見本用）

Semi-running Style Certificate
29 x 41cm

# 紅秋篆刻集 Koshu Seal Art Collection  (Designed and Carved by Koshu )

龍　DRAGON　(3.9x3.9cm)

鷺　RUN BIRD (4.0x4.0cm)

王 KING & 妃 QUEEN (1.9x1.9cm)

紅秋 Koshu (3x3cm)

明美 Akemi (3x3cm)

紅秋 Koshu (2.2x2.2cm)

紅秋之印 Koshu (4.4x4.4cm)

Y
(1.8x1.8cm)

紅秋 Koshu
(1.8x1.8cm)

紅秋 Koshu(2.2x2.2cm)

吉冨紅秋 (3.8x2.9cm)
Koshu Yoshidomi

真心(1.2x2.3)
True heart

長冨(1.2x2.3)
Long fortune

エネルギーの流れ
Spiral (4x4cm)

明美 (3.2x1.9cm)
Akemi

| | | |
|---|---|---|

## 紅秋書道歴        Koshu Calligraphy History

| | 紅秋書道歴 | Koshu Calligraphy History |
|---|---|---|
| APR 1975 | 鳳南書芸社<br>藤本青山書道教室に通い始める | Hounanshogeisha : Mr Seizan Fujimoto Calligraphy School |
| APR 1982 - | 代々木文化学園<br>日本文化書道協会に入会<br>西脇呉石の書を学ぶ | Registered at Yoyogi Bunka College in Tokyo, Japan Bunka Calligraphy Course, Learning Mr Goseki Nishiwaki Style |
| OCT 1991 | 日本文化書道協会、毛筆学会にて師範の<br>免許を取得<br>師青山より雅号『紅秋』を受理 | At Japan Bunka Calligraphy Course<br>Qualified as Calligraphy Teacher specializing in Brushes. Received Artist name " Koshu" |
| NOV 1991 | 山口県商工会議所のギャラリーにて<br>紅秋書道作品展を開催 | First Koshu Solo Art Exhibition at the Gallery in Yamaguchi Chamber of Commerce and Industry |
| SEP 1992 | ドリームハウス有限会社設立<br>紅秋書道教室開設 | Launch of company "Dream House" & Koshu Calligraphy School |
| OCT 1992 | 関西南画院入会<br>南画及び水墨画を学ぶ | Registered at Kansai Nanga College, Learning Nanga & Suiboku Painting |
| MAY 1993<br>- AUG 1994 | 日本書道揮毫協会に入会<br>賞状揮毫本科の全課程を受講 | Registered at Japan Calligraphy Kigo College, Take whole course in Certificates form |
| MAY 1994 | 日本書道揮毫協会にて資格師範の<br>認定を受ける | At Japan Calligraphy Kigo College, Qualified as Kigo Master |
| AUG 1994 | 日本書道揮毫協会にて資格賞状揮毫士教授の認定<br>を受ける | At Japan Calligraphy Kigo College, Qualified as Kigo Highest Master |
| SEP 1994<br>- DEC1995 | 鳳南書芸社にて篆刻及び表装課程を受講 | At Hounan Shogeisha, Took Seal Curving and Scroll Making Course |
| FEB 1995 | 山口県タナカギャラリーに作品を展示 | Exhibited Koshu Art at Tanaka Gallery in Yamaguchi |
| MAY 1995 | 山口県ギャラリー赤レンガに作品を展示 | Exhibited Koshu Art at Gallery Akarenga in Yamaguchi |
| FEB 1996 | 山口県タナカギャラリーに作品を展示 | Exhibited Koshu Art at Tanaka Galley in Yamaguchi |
| OCT 1997 -<br>SEP 1998 | 代々木文化学園、日本文化書道協会、<br>文化ペン字学会に入会 | Registered at Yoyogi Bunka College, Japan Bunka Calligraphy Course, Pen Writing |
| OCT 1998 | 日本文化書道協会、<br>文化ペン字学会にて師範免許取得 | Japan Bunka Calligraphy Course, Qualified as Calligraphy Teacher specializing in Pen Writing |
| FEB 2000 -<br>MAR2001 | 山口県農協印刷株式会社の専属揮毫士<br>として依頼の仕事に携わる | Worked as an excusive Kigo Master at Nokyo Printing Company |
| APR 2001 | ドリームハウス有限会社を廃業<br>渡英 | Closed the company "Dream House"<br>Moved to the UK |
| JUN 2001 | サウスナットフィールドにてエリザベス<br>女王６０年記念祭に書と水墨画を展示 | Exhibited Koshu Art at Queen Elizabeth II Golden Jubilee Cerebration Art and Crafts Exhibition in South Nutfield |
| SEP 2001 | イーストサリーカレッジにて日本書道及び水墨画<br>コースを担当 | Taught Japanese Calligraphy & Painting Course at the East Surrey College |
| SEP 2002 | 英国、紅秋書道教室ケイトラムを開設 | Started Koshu Calligraphy Class in Caterham |

| FEB 2004 | ブレッチングリー中央ギャラリーにて<br>紅秋書道作品展『真心』を開催 | Held Koshu Solo Japanese Art Exhibition<br>" Magokoro" at Centre Gallery at Bletchingley |
|---|---|---|
| APR 2004 | リングフィールドにて日本書道、水墨画の講演お<br>よびデモンストレーション実施 | Talk and Demonstration of Japanese Calligraphy and<br>Painting at Lingfield |
| MAY 2004 | 劇団の舞台道具として屏風を手掛ける | Commissioned Art Work for the Stage Set at the<br>Theatre |
| JUL 2006 -<br>AUG 2010 | 日本帰国<br>期間限定ペン字、書道教室開設 | Moving to Japan, teaching Brush and Pen Writing as<br>intensive course |
| OCT 2010 | 渡英<br>紅秋書道教室ケイトラム再開設 | Moving back to the UK, Start Koshu Calligraphy Class<br>again |
| FEB 2011 | リッチモンド日本食レストランの書画を<br>手掛ける | Commissioned Art Work, Calligraphy and Painting at<br>the Japanese Restaurant in Richmond, London |
| OCT 2011 | ケイトラム、ミラーセンターにて<br>紅秋書道教室、生徒の作品展を開催 | Koshu Japanese Art Students Exhibition at the Miller<br>Centre in Caterham |
| OCT 2012 | ケイトラム教室に併せキャンベリー教室<br>開設 | Open Camberley Koshu Calligraphy Classes as well<br>as Caterham Classses |
| NOV 2013 | ロンドンフレイムレスギャラリーにて<br>紅秋書道作品展『愛と夢』を開催<br>及び作品集『愛と夢』の発行 | Koshu Solo Japanese Art Exhibition "Love &<br>Dream"at Frameless Gallery in London<br>Publish the Koshu Art book "Love & Dream" |

# 紅秋に関わりのある書家　Direct Lineage for Koshu （暁風書院、近代書家系譜参考）

### Meikaku Kusakabe

日下部鳴鶴 (1838-1922) 明治新政府の内閣大書記官を勤め、退官後楊守敬の影響を受けて鳴鶴流を開いた。中村悟竹、巌谷一六と共に明治の三筆と呼ばれる近代書道の確立者の一人である。芸術家としても教育者としても多大な功績をあげたと称えて『日本近代書道の父』と評される。数多くの弟子を育成、現在でも彼の流派を受け継ぐ書道家は多い。

**Meikaku** was a Cabinet Diplomat of the New Government in the Meiji Period. After his retirement, he developed his own Meikaku style, influenced by a Chinese Calligrapher named **Yang Shoujing**. He became one of the three most influential calligraphers of the Meiji period, along with **Gochiku Nakamura** and **Ichiroku Iwaya**. He was named as the Father of Modern Japanese Calligraphy, and known as an artist as well as an educator. He trained a great many apprentices, so even now a lot of calligraphers follow his style.

### Kaikaku Niwa

丹波海鶴 (1863-1931) 日下部海鶴に師事。明治から大正にかけて活躍した書家で鄭道昭や初唐の楷書を基調とした海鶴の書風は海鶴流と称され一世を風靡した。比田井天来、近藤雪竹と共に書壇の双璧をもって目され、書道教育界に影響を持ち習字教科書の書風を改革して近代書道教育の発展に貢献した。

**Kaikaku** studied under **Meikaku Kusakabe**. His active period covered both the Meiji and Taisho period (late 19th century to the mid-1920s). He created his own style, based on **Zhèng Dàozhāo** style dating from sixth-century China, and the "Kaikaku Style" predominated all over Japan. He was one of the most charismatic calligraphers with **Tenrai Hirai** and **Secchiku Kondo**. He had great influence in the world of calligraphy and focused on developing the modern calligraphy education.

### Kakudo Arita

有田鶴堂 (1899-1974) 山口県長門市に生まれ大正9年上京し書家の第一人者、日下部鳴鶴の門を叩く。鳴鶴の紹介で丹波海鶴に師事し、書家として歩み始める。仮名においては小野鵞堂(仮名書道の祖と呼ばれる)と高塚竹堂に師事し、当時の一流の大家と交わり日本の教育書道の革新と実用書道、芸術書道の振興に貢献した。小学校教諭として転じる一方、萩に『暁風書院』を開設、後進の育成に精神的に取り組んだ。

**Kakudo** was born in Yamaguchi and went to **Meikaku Kusakabe's** school in Tokyo in the 9th year of Taisho. There, he studied under **Kaikaku Niwa** and became a professional calligrapher. In Kana style, he studied under **Chikudo Takatuki** who studied under **Gado Ono**, who was a historically well-known calligrapher in Kana style. Kakudo collaborated with other calligraphy experts and focused on innovating calligraphy education and also introducing calligraphy for both artistic uses and for writing. He opened his calligraphy school in Hagi and focused on training his successors as well as working as an elementary school teacher.

### Seizan Fujimoto

藤本青山 (1919-2004) 山口県に生まれ有田海鶴に師事。山口市に『鳳南書芸会』を開設し日本書道揮毫協会副会長を勤める。師、鶴堂の遺言で西脇呉石(日下部鳴鶴に師事)の書も学ぶようにと告げられ、呉石の書風と共に教育書道の基本練習に徹底した。『数理的結構法』を提唱し『美しい字』の探究に時間を惜しまず、一生涯を後進の育成に精進した。また表装の技術が達者で文化財の書作品の修復に貢献した。

**Seizan** was born in Yamaguchi and studied under **Kakudo Arita**. He opened the "Honanshogei School" and became a vice-president of Japan Calligraphy Kigo Association. Kakudo advised him to study the style of **Goseki Nishiwaki,** who also studied under **Meikaku Kusakabe**. Seizan focused on teaching the basic skills for beautiful writing. He used mathematical based proportions to achieve his beautiful calligraphy, which he developed into a book. He spent his life teaching and training his successors, and also used his great skill in scroll-making to contribute to the restoration of historically important works.

### Koshu Yoshidomi

吉冨紅秋 （ルーカス明美） (1967- ) 八歳で藤本青山の『鳳南書芸会』にて書を学び始める。師の指導のもと西脇呉石の書風を学びさらに多数の著名な書家の書風にも触れる。二十五歳で山口に紅秋書道教室を開設し、平成十四年より英国にて国際的に日本文化、芸術の紹介に積極的に取り組み、東洋と西洋の芸術をブレンドした独自の作品を制作する。

**Koshu** (Akemi) : At the age of 8, she started to learn calligraphy under **Seizan Fujimoto**. Under Seizan's guidance, she studied **Goseki Nishiwaki's** style and later on studied other well-known calligraphers' styles as well. At the age of 24, she opened "Koshu Calligraphy School" in Japan, and since 2002 she has been teaching and introducing Japanese Art internationally in the UK. She started to create her own style of art by blending the Eastern and Western cultures.

# 『愛と夢』

## 書との出逢い

　八歳になったある日『明美、今から藤本先生の所に書道を習いに行きなさい。智美 (姉) も壮克 (弟) も行くからこれを持って一緒に行きなさい。』といきなり書道道具セットを渡され、理由も分からず行く事になった。それが私の書との出逢いであり、藤本青山師匠との出逢いとなった。教室では毎月の課題作品が渡される。それが上手に書けた生徒は帰宅が許された。しかし私は一生懸命練習をするものの、なかなか先生から褒めてもらえず毎回居残り組。最終的にお情けの丸がもらえるまで何時間でも暗くなるまで練習を続けていた。数年後、気がついたら姉も弟も近所の子供たちもやめてしまい、私一人のみが教室に通っていた。しかし私は構わずひたすら練習を続けた。

　昭和四十二年私は山口県の小さな町で、平穏な家族のもとに生まれ深い愛情を受けながら何不自由無く育っていた。ところが突然、三歳の時に網膜芽細胞腫という病気にかかり、左目の視力を完全に失うことになってしまった。左右のバランス、前後の距離感がつかめず、衝突や転倒を頻繁に起こすようになり、傷が絶えない幼少の時を過ごしていた。家族は疲れやすく病気がちな私を心配し、また癌の再発の可能性も常に恐れ、頻繁な病院通いを余儀なくしていた。『人並みに不自由なく育ってくれれば良いのだけれど。』と、常に私のことを心配していた祖父、両親の気持ちを小さいながら感じていた。幼少の頃から自然と『人生の意味』を深く考えるようになっていた。祖父、両親を悲しませたくない、自分の命がいつ亡くなっても後悔のない生き方をしたいと、『できない。』という言葉は絶対に口にせず、勉強、運動全てにおいて時間の有る限り人の何倍もの努力を惜しまず、一瞬一瞬を精一杯生きることを当たり前のようにしていた。

## 雅号『紅秋』、大切な言葉

　実際には書道を始めた理由さえ知らず、書道に魅力を感じていた訳でもなかった。ただ師匠に上手に書けたと、褒めてもらいたいという思いのみが続ける理由だった。大阪での学生時代も、また海外旅行でも、常に筆を持ち続け何時間でも練習を重ね、師匠に送付し添削の依頼をしていた。徐々に好奇心が増してきて、所属していた東京の文化書道学会の検定試験にも真剣に取り組むようになり、二十三歳で師範免許取得の検定試験の段階にまできていた。その当時は正社員として会社勤務をしながら毎日勤務後はダンス教室に通い、週末はジャズバンドで歌う中で、睡眠時間を三、四時間に削り、食事もまともに摂らず、友人の誘いを断ることで時間を作り精一杯書の練習に励んでいた。両親は無理をしている私の体調をとても心配していたが、ただ黙って見守ってくれていた。

明美二十歳成人式
Akemi 20 years old

　しかし検定作品を練習して師匠の所に指導を受けに伺うと、書を見せる前にいきなり玄関先でとめられ『見るに至らん！帰れ！』と何度も追い返された。車に戻ると悔し涙が溢れ出た。精一杯の努力も認められず、作品も受け取られず玄関先で追い返えされ、一体私の何が不足しているのか、その時の未熟な私には全く理解できずにいた。途方に暮れる暗中模索の日々が数ヶ月続いた。悔しすぎて諦められず、意地になって練習を続け師匠に見せに何度も足を運んだ。そんなある日、師匠がやっと言葉をくれた。『明美さんよ、百枚二百枚練習したからと練習したつもりになるではない！何千枚と練習して初めて何かが見えてくる。まだまだ心の修行が足りておらん。我欲で書く字は見るに至らん。無心で取り組めた時、初めて心が筆を動かし、心を描く字につながる！』今までの私の未熟で傲慢な態度を指摘してもらい、書に取り組む姿勢、心の修行の重要さを教えてもらった。まさしく『書は心』だった。帰宅して今までの練習作品を全て捨てると同時に我欲と傲慢さを捨てる心の修行を始めた。

　数ヶ月が過ぎたある日、今まで体感した事の無い新鮮な感覚を味わった。それは私の心と白い紙の間に何も無い、まるで広大な宇宙に包まれた感覚だった。まさに筆と心の一体化に心が満たされた。すぐに作品を持って車を走らせた。驚いた事になぜか師匠は玄関で私を待っていた。『明美さん、良く来たな、あがりなさい。その作品を壁に張りなさい。』と初めて師匠が検定用の作品を見てくれた。『明美さんよ、良くここまでついてきたなあ。しっかりと褒めてやるぞ。良く頑張った。良い作品が書けておる。これで良い。』八歳で書を始め、十六年後初めて師匠から褒めてもらえた。そして初めて師匠の前で泣いた。『明美さん、良く聞きなさい。今、本当の書の道を歩む時が来た。これからが本当の勉強が始まる。私の師匠の有田鶴堂がくれた遺言と同じ事を伝える。書の師範になれたからと言って、まだ先生とは言われん。絵筆も握り、篆刻も彫り、表装もしなさい。賞状書きの版下も立派にできるようにならんといけん。そして初めて先生と呼べる。様々な芸術にも触れることも大切。一生自分の勉強に費やす時間を惜しんではならん。大きな展示会などの競展には絶対に逆上せてはいけん。賞などは必要ない。基本を忘れることはならん。良いか、明美さん。』と師匠からの大事な言葉を受け取った。同時に、青々とした広大な山（青山）の中で美しく鮮やかな紅葉のように、ひときわ輝く情熱的な魅力ある女性書道家になれるようにとの想いを込めて、書道家『紅秋』と言う雅号を受け取った。その翌月には地元山口県で最初の紅秋書道展を開催した。

『小学校が始まって、バランスがとれず字が上手に書けない明美が可哀想でね。なんとかしてやりたいと思って書道教室に行かせたのよ。 明美が行くのを嫌がらないように智美と壮克も一緒に行かせたの。でも師範になるまで良く頑張ったね。』と初めて母が私にきっかけの理由を話してくれた。

## 本格的な勉強、人生の大変化

本格的に書の道を歩み始めた。正社員の仕事もしながら、師から全てを習得したいと、曜日や時間構わず師の所へ足を運び学んだ。絵筆を握り、篆刻を彫り、伝統的な表装の仕方も学び、文化書道ペン字部門で師範免許を所得し、東京の揮毫協会にも入会し賞状書きの師範免許も取得した。平成五年、師からその年の秋には書道教室を開校してよいとの許可を受けた。それを機会に会社を退職し、渡英することを決心した。以前からイギリスの歴史や英語に強く惹かれ渡英を夢見ていた。師も私の渡英には人生の視野を広げ新たな感覚を養う為にも大賛成だった。半年間ロンドンの語学学校に通い、夜はホームステイ先の部屋にこもり夜中遅くまで筆を持ち、練習に励み、頻繁に日本の師匠に作品を送り指導を受けた。

ドリームハウス有限会社(紅秋書道教室&英会話教室)
Dream House (English and Koshu Calligraphy School)

帰国後『紅秋書道教室』を、英会話教室と併せ『ドリームハウス有限会社』として開校が実現した。そして英国滞在中に出逢ったイギリス人男性と翌年結婚、日本での結婚生活が始まった。主婦として、二百五十人前後の生徒が通う教室経営者として、そして書道家としての活動とかなり充実した多忙な日々を過ごしていた。四年後には待望の長女を出産し、これ以上望む物は無く、言葉では表現できないほどの至福感を味わっていた。

ところが、突然想像もしていなかった悲劇が家族を襲った。主人が身体中からの痛みを訴えるようになり、数ヶ月の検査の結果、癌の末期だと診断された。闘病生活五ヶ月後には私と一歳の娘を遺し、主人はこの世を去ってしまった。至福の絶頂期から、いきなり谷底に落とされたショックは大き過ぎた。五年間のあまりにも短い結婚生活、娘が生まれて家族として過ごせたのは、たったの一年。主人の死が受け止められず、完全に人生を見失ってしまった。『もしも、主人の人生がこんなに短いのだと知っていれば、何よりも彼との時間を優先し大切にしていたのに…。未来があると思っていたから仕事も書道も頑張ってきたのに…。』仕事や書道に費やしていた時間を後悔し、書道の作品制作に夢中に取り組んでいた自分を責めずにはいられなかった。苦しくて呼吸さえできない、筆が全く持てない自分になってしまった。『もう書はしない…。』完全に暗闇の中に入り込んでしまった。誰の言葉も聞こえない、筆も持てない、世界中の全てを嫌悪し、希望、未来、夢、全てが消え去り、涙が枯れるまで泣き通した。

笑顔の無いまま教室の経営を続けていた一年後のある日、無理が祟り突然倒れ病院に運ばれた。今までずっと黙って見守ってくれていた父が初めて言葉をくれた。『英会話や書道の生徒は別の先生が探せる。でも娘にとっての母親は明美だけだ。生きていかないと。娘の為にも笑顔を取り戻さないとな。イギリスに行っておいで。行きたいんだろう？』亡主人が遺した『娘に英国を知って育ち、英国の祖父母と触れ合う時間を与え、英国の教育を受けさせたい。』との願い。その時の私には、主人のこの想いを叶えることのみが唯一私の生きる希望の光だったのを父は知っていた。

## 渡英、英国での人生

主人との死別から二年半後、小さな娘と二人での渡英を決心し、熱い思いを込めて立ち上げ、運営していた書道及び英会話教室『ドリームハウス (有) 』を廃業にする事を決めた。渡英後は英国でカウンセリングを受け、亡主人の家族、友人から受ける愛情と励ましのお陰で徐々に自分を責める事を止め、未来から差し込む光に気付くようになり、筆を持つことを自分自身に許せるように立ち直ってきた。そして英国で書道教室の再開ができるようになった。独特な日本文化に魅了され、その技術を習得したいと、真剣に練習を積み重ねていく熱心な生徒たちの姿に励まされ、私もようやく自分の作品制作にも取り組めるようになってきた。想いが溢れ出る、白い紙の上で筆が舞う、感じるままに表現し続けた。生きる喜びを感じ始めた。

その翌年平成十六年二月、英国での最初のソロ個展『真心』の開催が実現し、多くの人が個展会場に足を運んでくれた。『作品を見せてくれてありがとう、是非このような日本文化に触れられる機会をもっと与えて欲しい。』と 温かい感想の言葉を頂いた。日本の芸術、書道に関する講演会の依頼も受け、二度書きができない、一筆で全てを表現する技術、心の向け方、和紙と墨の関わり合いへの理解を通して広がる美の世界を、実技を兼ねて紹介した。 英国で日本書道家としての活動に深い喜びと達成感を感じるようになり、お陰でやっと私らしい笑顔が戻って来るようになった。作品依頼の仕事も次から次へと増え、忙しい日々を過ごし始め、書道家として再軌道に乗り始めた。

## 更なる別れ

しかし英国で娘と二人での生活は簡単ではなく、特に医療事情に無知だった私は一旦体調を崩すと病状を悪化させてしまうことが多かった。『ママも死んで一人ぼっちになってしまう。』と娘をかなり不安にさせてしまったようだった。その年の春から数ヶ月間にかけて病気が続き悪化した為、最終的に日本に帰国が余儀なくされ、日本で手術と治療を受ける事になった。手術後回復を待っている間、青山師匠から電話をもらった。『明美さん、帰国の間五回ほど来なさい。もう

一つだけ教えておく事がある。イギリスで必ず役に立つ、簡単な近代表装の仕方を教えておきたい。』と。当時師匠は重病で寝込んでいたが、私の到着五分前には寝床から起き上がり二階の工房に上がり二時間ばかりの指導をしてくれた。本来なら起き上がれる身体ではなかったようだ。『もう疲れたから今日はここまで。また次回にこの次を教えるから来なさい。』と。そして最後の五回目の指導が終わったとき『明美さん、私が教えられる全てのことは教えてきた。これからは自信を持って世界に書道家として出て行きなさい。本当にここまで良くついてきたな。どこに出しても恥ずかしくない私の自慢の弟子だ。一生、基本を忘れず、勉強をし続けなさい。私もまだまだ勉強することがある。気をつけてイギリスに帰りなさいよ。』と。そしてそれが師匠からの最後の言葉となった。私が英国に飛び立った翌日、師匠は倒れ病院に運ばれ、数週間後にこの世を去った。『心に届く美しい字』をとことん追求し、高いレベルまで私を育てる事に情熱を注ぎ、人生最後の瞬間まで徹底した指導を愛情込めてしてくれた。そんな師に出逢えた事に感謝せずにはいられなかった。師匠の想いや言葉を忘れることなく、次は私から私の生徒へ技術、知識、愛を与え続ける事、そして私の作品を世の中に出していく事、それが師に対しての恩返しになるのだと心に固く誓った。帰国後、体調の回復をみながら書道活動に更に真剣に取り組み始めた。

　落ち着いた人生が送りたいと願う一方、現実はなぜか真反対。次から次へと困難が私を待っていた。別の治療を受けるため再度日本へ帰国が余儀なくされた。日本で二、三ヶ月入院し治療を受け、更に三ヶ月の療養後、やっと英国帰国が可能となった。しかし英国へ戻った矢先、深い愛情で励まし支えてくれ、私の書を自慢してくれていた大好きな父が膵臓癌の末期だと診断されたと、悲しい知らせを受けた。闘病生活をしている父と離れている事がどうしても耐えられず、悩んだ結果、英国での生活を完全に諦めることを決心し、平成十八年の夏、日本に引越し帰国をした。『明美の今度の個展には行くからな！』と約束したのに、叶う前に父はこの世を去ってしまった。私を置いて大切な人が皆逝ってしまう悲しみをどう隠したら良いのか、もはや分からなくなってしまった。

## 新たな出逢い、夢の実現

　進むべき道は見えるものの、実際は心も身体も疲れきってしまい、さまよう月日を過ごした。日本からは英国が遥か遠い国に感じた。そんな時、英国で私の帰国を待ってくれていた生徒からの熱心な想いを受け、書道家としての活動に深い喜びを感じられるのは、もはや日本ではなく英国でしかないと再確認し勇気を与えてもらえた。そして四年間の日本滞在に終止符を打つ決心ができた。もう日本に戻る事は無いだろう。

　渡英後すぐに書道教室を再開した。そして日本帰国前から約束していた生徒の作品展準備に集中し、一年後実現が可能となった。お陰で素晴らしい作品展が開催でき、多くの方から高い評価を頂き、更に生徒と共に力強く歩み始めた。同時に、紅秋のホームページの開設にも取り組み、開設直後にはロンドンに近い日本食レストランでの書の依頼の仕事の連絡を受け、運命的な新たな出逢いに恵まれた。また距離を超えてあちこちから書道作品の依頼も殺到するようになり、『明美』としてまた書道家『紅秋』としての希望に満ちた新たな人生が始まった。

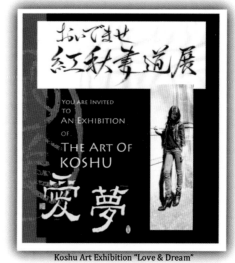

Koshu Art Exhibition "Love & Dream"
In 2013 at Frameless Gallery in London

　今年平成二十五年は、長年待望してきた夢の実現に向けてスタートした。ここまで長く遠い困難な道のりだった。その間温めてきた想いは深い。筆を持ち白い紙に向かう度に、亡主人、師匠、父からの深い愛情を感じる。宇宙、太陽、月からのエネルギーと愛が私の『力の源』となり、娘や日本と英国の家族そして世界中の友人からの深い愛情が私の『勇気』となる。小さい頃から感じてきたもの、見てきたもの、体験してきたもの、そして今イメージするものが、東洋と西洋、過去と未来、伝統と飛躍と重なり合い調和を取りながら私の身体と心を通して表現されていく。胸が熱くなり愛が溢れ出る。私の筆が舞い始める。舞い続ける。

　言葉を越え、国境を越え、作品の前に立って私からのメッセージを人々に感じてもらえること、それが私の夢。平成二十五年、紅秋書道展『愛と夢』、そこには今まで支えてくれた師匠、家族、友人へ、そして会場に足を運んでくださる方々、作品集を通して私を知ってくださる方々、皆さんのお陰で実現が可能となった。深い感謝の気持ちを込めて心から『ありがとう。』

　この瞬間からが、また私の新たなスタート。師からの言葉を守り精進し続け、命の与えてもらえる限り『明美』を表現し『紅秋』として作品を完成させていきたい。

平成二十五年十一月
紅秋　(ルーカス明美)

# "Love and Dream"

## Encounter the Calligraphy World

The day I turned eight, my mother suddenly told me "Akemi, go to Mr Fujimoto's calligraphy school from now. Your sister and brother are going with you, so take this bag with you." Without being told why, I was given a set of calligraphy equipment and was sent to the calligraphy school. This was how I encountered the calligraphy world under Mr Seizan Fujimoto's guidance. At his school, we were all given a monthly sample piece of work. We were only given permission to leave his lesson once we were able to accomplish a piece of work good enough for him. Despite long hours of hard work, unfortunately my writing was never good enough for me to leave. Consequently leaving me no option but to stay there alone, every lesson till it got dark. In the end, I was always given his sympathetic permission to go home. Several years later, all my friends, my sister and my brother had already quit learning calligraphy. But I didn't want to give up; and I carried on.

I was born in a small town in southern Japan in 1967, and I was brought up with the utmost care and deepest love from my family. However, at the age of three, I was diagnosed as having eye cancer. I lost my left eyesight completely, which caused difficulties in balance. This resulted in frequent falls and collisions. With the anxiety and fear about the recurrence of my cancer and also my physical weakness, I was taken to the hospital frequently. Since this young age, I had constantly felt my grandfather and parents' anxiety and sympathy towards me. They doubted whether I would ever be able to develop and mature without any disabilities or difficulties. Yet I promised myself to never to say the word "I can't!" and never to give up, dedicating myself to every opportunity I had. I knew I could make them happier and proud of having me as their daughter. But there was another reason: I somehow felt my life would be very short and therefore I wanted to pursue "the meaning of life" and achieve something worthwhile, so I could leave without any regrets. This is when I started to wonder deeply about the meaning of life. I realised that every single moment was a gift that I should treasure, bringing out the best in me: to devote yourself to everything.

## "KOSHU" and an Important Message

I had no idea why I was suddenly sent to calligraphy school, nor why I kept practising without any interest in it at that time. The only reason for carrying on was so that one day, I could be rewarded with a complement from my teacher. Wherever I was, in Osaka at University or travelling to different countries, I never stopped practising and always sent my artwork to my teacher. I gradually became more and more interested in calligraphy and more serious about grading at the Bunka Calligraphy School in Tokyo. This led me to the last stage at challenging the exam to become a calligraphy teacher at the age of 23. I was working full-time for a company, teaching dancing in the evening, singing in the jazz band at the weekends, and so made my time for calligraphy by eating less, sleeping only 3-4 hours a day, and forgetting my social life. My parents were so worried about my health, but they continued to support me, as they knew my dedication to calligraphy.

明美 23 歳山口秋吉台にて
Akemi 23 At Akiyoshi Hill

In spite of my great effort in practising, my artwork was never good enough. Every single time I went to my teacher in order to present my artwork, he stood at the front door and said, "It is not worth looking at! Go home." His rejections were relentless and endless. I didn't understand why he was so harsh to me, leaving me lost and hopeless, but I didn't want my endless practice to be worthless. I was so determined; I kept practising and visiting him. One day, when I went to see him, he obliged, "Akemi, listen. Repeating only a hundred times is just useless. A thousand repetitions finally enables you to understand the important things. Your mind has not been trained. All your work has the wrong mindset, and is not worth looking at. When you write with the right mind, you will finally be able to control your brush and express your feelings." I realised and learnt for the first time how calligraphy was not just a painting nor a collection of words. The saying "Calligraphy is the mind" became true to me. His harsh words astonished and affected me. As soon as I arrived home I threw away all my practice papers; and at the same time threw away my arrogance and greed. I started to look into my inner sense of self. It was almost hurtful, and took time to go through with. But one day I felt everything change; I felt the movement of the universe around me, whilst my brush danced on the paper. I immediately visited my teacher to show my new work. To my surprise, he was waiting for me outside the house, and he welcomed me with these words: "Akemi, I was waiting for you. Well done, you can come up now. Put your artwork on the wall here, I would love to look at it! Akemi, I am so proud of you for following my teaching for such a long time, and I give you my first compliment. You have produced a beautiful piece of YOUR art, and this is what I have been waiting for." Sixteen years had passed since I started to learn Calligraphy under him, and at last I was given these words. I cried in front of him for the first time. "Now, Akemi, listen very carefully. Today, you finally started to walk the path of real Calligraphy. The true study has just started. This is the same message my master, Mr Kakudo Arita, gave me. Even though you are now qualified as a calligraphy teacher, you should not claim that you are one. After you can hold paintbrushes, carve seals, make scrolls, and write certificate forms, then, and only then should you call yourself a calligraphy teacher. You should never stop studying and train for the rest of your life. Never try to enter the big competitions. You do not need awards, as the most important thing is being humble and never forgetting the beginner's mind. Never forget what I have told you, Akemi."

I was then honoured to receive my artist's name "Koshu", meaning "Red Autumn", symbolic of the passionate beauty with connotations to the diversity of colours in Japanese Autumn, whilst he wished for me to become a passionate and attractive female calligrapher. Contrasting rapidly is my teacher's name "Seizan" meaning "Blue Mountain"; symbolic of his strength and respectability. Next month, I held my first Koshu Solo Art Exhibition in Yamaguchi prefecture.

My mother also finally described her feelings to me saying, "Akemi, honestly, I felt so sorry for you, as you struggled to write in the beginning at school. You just couldn't get the balance right because of your eye. So I decided to send you to the calligraphy school to help with your problems. I just sent your sister and brother just in case you refused to go. I am so proud of you for never giving up and accomplishing the title as a teacher."

## Focusing on learning & Big Change in my life

My real training only started then. I was determined to learn everything from my teacher. Still carrying on with my full time job, I visited my teacher whenever I could; no matter what time or what day it was. I kept trying to make as much time as possible to paint Sumie (Japanese ink painting), to learn how to carve seals, to learn how to make traditional scrolls, to gain a teaching qualification specializing in pen writing, and also to register at a different school in Tokyo to learn writing for certificate forms.

I was given approval from my teacher to open my own calligraphy school in 1992. I decided to quit my job and travel to the UK to study English before opening the school in autumn. I was somehow so fascinated by England, as if my soul was pulled there. My teacher was also enthusiastic for me to go abroad in order to widen my mind and understand more. I went to the language school in London for 5 months, and every night I stayed in my room at the host family and kept practising calligraphy to send my work to my teacher in Japan.

After returning to Japan, I set up the company called "Dream House" a language and calligraphy school. The following year, I married an English man whom I met during my last stay. Our married life started in Japan. Being a wife, an owner of a school with 250 students, and being a professional calligrapher, my life was extremely busy and fulfilled. After 4 years of our marriage, we were blessed with a baby daughter, making my life almost perfect and I had never felt happier.

However, the blissful time didn't last long. Suddenly, a tragedy attacked us and my happy life turned into the saddest and darkest life. My husband started to suffer from crucial pain all over his body, and several months later, he was diagnosed with terminal cancer. Whilst he still fought for me and our daughter, he only had several months left; sadly he passed away leaving me and our one year old daughter behind. It was only a five-year long marriage, and we only had one year of family life. I was completely devastated and lost my way. "If only I had known his life was so short, I would have spent more time with him and treasured his presence more. Why did I spend so much time working and focusing on my art?" I thought our life together would have lasted many years. I couldn't stop regretting what I had done and I couldn't stop blaming myself for working so hard and focusing on my art. I even felt guilty for enjoying art. Suddenly I became unable to hold any brushes; "I will never do my art again…" I put myself into a deep dark world: I couldn't hear anyone's voice. I couldn't smile. I hated everything in this world. There was no 'hope', 'dream' nor 'future' anymore. I saw no ending to this dark tunnel, and saw no hope of light. Tears filled my eyes, as I wished for my husband to come back to me.

My sense of time had disappeared as months and months passed without any joy; one year passed. I was making myself very ill, and one day when I was carried to hospital after fainting, my father finally opened his mouth and gave me his words; "Akemi, your students can find another teacher, but you are the only mother for your daughter. You need to live for her, and you need to get back your smile for her. Why don't you go to England? I know you would love to go there, wouldn't you?" He knew about my hidden feelings of wanting to make my husband's wish come true: to bring up our daughter knowing England, being close to her English grandparents, and giving her a chance to have an English education. To make his wish come true was the only hope and purpose for me to live at that time.

## Life in the UK

Two years after my husband's death, following my father's advice, I decided to move to the UK with my daughter, closing my treasured school in Japan. It wasn't easy to live in a different country on my own with a small child, but the support I received from my counsellor, my husband's family and friends helped me through. I was able to stop blaming myself, and started to look to the future. Finally after the few years, I could hold a brush again and also managed to start calligraphy classes. My students were so fascinated with the uniqueness of Japanese culture and art, and became so enthusiastic and dedicated to practice and learn the techniques. Their humble attitude cheered me up amazingly and brought my passion for art back; facing the white paper and holding my brush, I enjoyed the feeling of my heart moving as my brushes danced again.

紅秋書道展『真心』2004　英国サリー州
Koshu Art Exhibition "Magokoro" 2004 in Surrey

In February 2004, I held a Koshu Solo Calligraphy Art Exhibition entitled "Magokoro" (Sincerely from my heart). I was so touched by having so many visitors with great feedback: "Thank you so much for showing us your work. We would love to have more opportunities to see Japanese culture and your beautiful art." When I was invited to give a talk about Japanese Art, I introduced the special technique and a way to train your own mind. I also explained the harmony between the paper and ink, so that they can produce a beautiful piece of artwork. I felt a great joy and satisfaction in introducing Japanese art and culture, and finally my smile started to come back to me. With many-commissioned artworks, my life as a calligrapher finally started to bloom after the hard time.

## Another Farewell

Unfortunately, my life wasn't so simple as I had wished. I became seriously ill, and after a few months of receiving medical treatment here, I decided to fly back to Japan for a special treatment. My poor small daughter looked after me anxiously, knowing that if I died, she would be left behind alone. In summer 2004, I was in a hospital in Japan, receiving treatment and an operation. During my stay, my calligraphy teacher gave me a phone call. "Akemi, come to see me 5 times while you are in Japan. There is one more thing I want to teach you and I believe it will be very useful for you in the UK. Come here to learn modern scroll making." At that time, my teacher had been in bed suffering from a severe illness. I was still convalescing, but I pushed myself to follow his instructions. Five minutes before my arrival, he got up from his bed, and walked upstairs to his studio. There he taught me the method of modern scroll making. Doctors couldn't believe that he managed to get up to give me lessons despite his poor health. "Akemi, I am tired now, today's lesson has finished. Come here another day again." After finishing 5 sessions with me, he spoke to me, "Akemi, I have taught you everything possible. I can proudly tell you that you can be very confident about your skills and go out into the world as a professional calligrapher. You have dedicated yourself to me sincerely and what you have achieved is incredible! I am very proud of you as my apprentice. I have no doubt in you as a calligrapher. But never forget your beginner's mind, and never stop learning. I have still so many things I want to study after I get better. Please look after yourself and have a safe journey back to the UK." These words became his last message to me. The next day after I left to the UK, he was carried to hospital and a few weeks later, he passed away. The appreciation I carry within me towards him is indescribable and endless; all that he gave to me with his deep and endless love. I will never forget him and what he taught me. Now was the time for me to give everything by doing the same things for my students; giving my skill, knowledge and love. And I swore to myself that I would try my best to show my art to people from all over the world one day.

Despite my wish to settle back down in the UK, many difficulties awaited me one after another. I had to return to Japan once again for a different medical treatment and so spent several months in hospital. A few months after my recovery in Japan, I finally went back to the UK. However, soon I was informed with devastating news about my father...who always gave me his love and support in everything I did, and was so proud of me and what I had achieved. He was diagnosed with terminal pancreatic cancer. I was completely devastated. I couldn't bear being apart from my father especially when he was going to die. And so after much consideration, I finally decided to give up living in the UK and move back to Japan. I made a promise to him to have my art exhibition in Japan soon, and he promised to live longer in order to make it. But sadly our promises were broken. He passed away before the exhibition. I couldn't deal with the feeling of emptiness and loneliness, knowing that the people I loved so much disappeared out of my life.

## My Dream Coming True

リッチモンドの日本食レストラン、依頼された紅秋書、画作品
Koshu's Art at the Japanese Restaurant in Richmond,
Restaurant was designed & built by Steve Howie

Although inside, I knew the path to walk, I was almost too exhausted both physically and emotionally to move towards my future. I felt England was too far away for me. Yet my UK students' feelings and dedications towards me reminded me that my heart belonged in the UK, and I would be much more fulfilled in the UK as a Calligrapher. Four years passed in Japan, and I finally made my decision to go back to the UK and live there for good.

Back in the UK, I started to focus on organizing students' art exhibition as I had promised before. All my students produced fantastic work and we were so pleased to have so many wonderful comments about the exhibition; it fulfilled my decision of coming back to the UK. As soon as I created a website entitled for Japanese calligraphy, I was asked to do many commissions. And this also led me to meet someone who was looking for me for a long time. My new life as Akemi as well as a calligrapher, Koshu, finally started.

2013: this year I started by focusing on making my dream come true, and the time finally came to me after long and hard journey. Every time I hold my brush, my heart is filled with the love from my late husband, my teacher and my father. The energy from the universe gives me 'strength', and the love from my daughters, my family and friends give me 'courage'. All that I have felt, seen and experienced in the past, can now be expressed with my feelings and sense of self in the present, to produce work for the future. My art consists of a mixture of the Eastern and Western culture, past and present feelings, and the traditional and contemporary calligraphy. All together express my heart and make my brush gracefully dance on the surface of the paper. My dream is to send my love and message through my art to everyone who visits my gallery.

Koshu Solo Art Exhibition "Love and Dream" 2013 came true, thanks to the support from all those around me. I would love to give my sincere gratitude and appreciation to you all. Thank you so much. This moment is my new start, and I will never forget the message from my teacher to carry on achieving and I would love to express myself and produce Koshu Art Work as long as my life is given.

Koshu (Akemi Lucas)
November 2013

# 『真心を込めて』 *Sincerely from my Heart*

32 x 25 cm

明美 Akemi 2013

紅秋作品集『愛と夢』の制作に携わってくれた娘マチルダ、ステーブ、ジェニーありがとう。
そして影でいつも支え励ましてくれている私の家族、友人、生徒、大切な皆さんのお陰で作品集を仕上げることができました。
真心を込めてありがとう。

紅秋（明美）2013

Thank you so much, Matilda, Steve and Jenny, for helping me to create this art book "Love and Dream", and thank you so much, my family, my friends and my students, for always supporting me and encouraging me.

Thank you all sincerely from my heart.

Koshu : Akemi 2013

**Published by Koshu Publishing**

ISBN 978-0-9927332-0-9

**Koshu Art Book "Love & Dream" 2013**

**Koshu Japanese Art Calligraphy**

紅秋　Koshu　(Akemi Lucas)

Please contact for commissioned Artwork & Seals and also for Japanese Art Course：

07713 113269

http://koshujapaneseart.co.uk